Motherhood

RESOURCES FOR BIBLICAL LIVING

Bitterness: The Root That Pollutes

Deception: Letting Go of Lying

Divorce: Before You Say "I Don't"

Fear: Breaking Its Grip

In-Laws: Married with Parents

Judgments: Rash or Righteous

Manipulation: Knowing How to Respond

Motherhood: Hope for Discouraged Moms

Problems: Solving Them God's Way

Self-Image: How to Overcome Inferiority Judgments

Motherhood

Hope for Discouraged Moms

BRENDA PAYNE

P&R PUBLISHING
P.O. BOX 817 • PHILLIPSBURG • NEW JERSEY 08865-0817

Printed in the United States of America

Library of Congress Cataloging-in-Publication Data

Payne, Brenda.
 Motherhood : hope for discouraged moms / Brenda Payne.
   p. cm. — (Resources for biblical living)
 Includes bibliographical references.
 ISBN 978-1-59638-169-8 (pbk.)
  1. Christian mothers—Religious life. 2. Motherhood—Religious aspects—Christianity. 3. Hope—Religious aspects—Christianity. 4. Encouragement—Religious aspects—Christianity. I. Title.
     BV4529.18.P39 2009
     248.8'431—dc22

                    2009024294

CHANCES ARE, you've picked up this booklet because you are feeling down, discouraged, or hopeless. Maybe you are overwhelmed with the heavy responsibilities of parenthood. The issues are growing weightier, and it feels like the future well-being of your child lies squarely on your shoulders. You might be going through the heartaches associated with a stubborn or rebellious child—even a willful two-year-old can bring a mother to her knees. Or you could simply be worn down from the daily grind of motherhood. You have made a million decisions concerning the life of your child and have given countless instructions. You are weary, and you don't see the fruitfulness you would expect from your tireless efforts. Discouragement has set in and is robbing you of your joy.

You are a mother, and your very title describes who you are. A mother is one who gives life. But these days, far from feeling like a life giver, you feel drained of life. Perhaps you are looking around at all the other "good" Christian mothers with their "good" Christian children and wondering, "What's wrong with me and my kids? How could I be failing at one of the most important things in all of life—parenthood? How could I mess up something I was so looking forward to doing?"

In your despair you might be tempted to think, "God made a mistake when he picked me to be a mother. I'm not cut out for this job." I can assure you, Christian mother, on the authority of God's Word, that the Lord doesn't make mistakes! If he has gifted you with children, then he has called you to the "good work" of motherhood (Eph. 2:10). And if he has called you, he will give you the equipment to get the job done (2 Peter 1:3).

Motherhood is a daunting task and an overwhelming responsibility. This is especially true of mothers who seek to diligently teach and train their children in God's Word and his ways and to instill in them the desire to love God with all their hearts. Amy Carmichael, a missionary to India who saved orphaned children from Hindu temple prostitution, said of such faithful Christian mothers, "We ask far more than the usual of our boys and girls, and this way of working asks far more of us."[1]

Consider this about your present despair: Your feelings could be an indicator that you are indeed asking "more than the usual" of your children. Perhaps you are taking God's call to motherhood as seriously as you should and are pouring your heart and soul into the task. In the process, you have been overwhelmed because this way of working asks far more of you than you can give in your own strength.

On the other hand, maybe you haven't given your mothering responsibilities the priority in your life they should have. You haven't fulfilled God's command to teach and train your children according to Scripture (Deut. 6:5–7). Maybe you haven't taken your job as seriously as you wish you had, and now you are suffering the consequences.

You Are Not Alone

Whatever circumstances have brought you to this point, you now desire to find answers to your parenting problems and hope for your discouragement. Let me encourage you that you are right where God wants you to be! He has your attention; open your ears and your heart wide to his counsel. First, notice what the Bible says about your trouble. "No temptation has seized you except what is common to man. And God is faithful; he will not let you be tempted beyond what you can bear. But when you are

1. Quoted in Elisabeth Elliot, *A Chance to Die* (Ada, MI: Revell, 2005).

tempted, he will also provide a way out so that you can stand up under it" (1 Cor. 10:13).

Let's dissect this encouraging verse. The word for *temptation* in this context can also mean "trial." The Greek word has the basic meaning of trying, testing, or proving. The apostle Paul, who penned this verse, was no stranger to trials. His Christian life was full of trouble! Of course, trials often provide opportunities to be tempted to sin. It is safe to assert, then, that every test from the devil's point of view is a temptation, and every temptation from God's point of view is a test.

Are the trials and temptations of parenting crushing and crippling you? Are you ready to give up or give in? Have you considered running away from home? (I mean it—I have!) Believe me, you are not alone.

Paul understood that neither his sufferings nor his temptations were unique. You need to understand this too. There is no problem in your current parenting situation that has not been common to mothers throughout the ages. I like to remind myself, "No temptation has seized you except what is common to every mom!" What does "common" mean? Widespread, ordinary, regular, familiar, universal, and frequent—these words describe your trial. It is important for you to remember this. Of course, your situation probably has a few unique elements, but fundamentally "there is nothing new under the sun" (Eccl. 1:9). If you believe you are the only Christian mother struggling with these issues, then you will be more easily discouraged. Defeatism thrives in isolation. In light of this verse, you should assume that other mothers are struggling too and should take courage, holding on to the hope that God has a plan to help you.

Not only is your trial *common to man*, it is one of the original struggles of the human race. Mothering woes go back as far as Eve. You might think that in an effort to encourage procreation the Bible would begin with a "happily ever after" story about marriage and children. But God does not attempt to hide the hardships of parenting in a fallen world. The very first example of mothering portrays the reality of sinners parenting sinners. Eve experienced tremendous heartache with her first sons; remember that Cain, Eve's firstborn, was exiled for murdering her younger son, Abel. Stop and ponder this for a moment. Envy, jealousy, and murder—these acts of treachery characterize the first mothering moments in history. There's certainly not much in this story to get you excited about motherhood!

Like Eve, you are raising children in a sin-laden world. As a result, you will regularly encounter hardship in your interaction with others. Furthermore, when God pronounced his curse on Eve, it directly impacted those dearest to her. "To the woman he said, 'I will greatly increase your pains in childbearing; with pain you will give birth to children. Your desire will be for your husband, and he will rule over you'" (Gen. 3:16). Some commentators interpret this curse to be a reference not only to the physical pain of labor and delivery, but also to the continued heartache a mother experiences over her children.

When you truly grasp the devastating toll that sin has taken on your ability to love God and your neighbor, you will not be surprised by the adversity associated with parenting. In fact, considering your own sin, the sins of your children, influences from the world, and Satan, it is utterly amazing that you can find one ounce of satisfaction in the parenting process! Job recognized the inevitability of trouble in this life. "Yet man is born to trouble as surely as sparks fly upward" (Job 5:7). I have heard it said that "parenting is the hardest job you will ever love." It is so very true! Therefore, expect trouble.

While we must expect trouble, we must not miss the promises. In the midst of this turmoil, God gave Eve hope. He gave her another son, the promise of a Savior, and redemption. Remember that God is faithful! He was faithful to Eve after her failure and sin and the sin of her children, and he will be faithful to you. He will not give you more than you can handle. Are you feeling like you can't handle your present trial? God promises that you

8

can—not because you are smart enough, strong enough, or wise enough to do anything on your own, but because he is faithful. What he says is true; what he says, he will do. God will provide the means to handle any and all troubles that come your way. He might be pleased to deliver you from your circumstances by changing your child's heart, or he might give you the ability to suffer or struggle through the trial by changing your heart.

What do you think upheld Eve through those dark days of parenting? I can't wait to ask her myself, but I feel certain she will say that it was her hope in the promises of God (Heb. 11:1–2, 39). My dear friend, remembering God's promises will get you through your dark parenting moments. You will need to know and cling to the truths of God's Word. Let's look at some truths that will anchor your soul during the storms of motherhood.

Confronting Your Failures

The discouragement you feel as a mother has probably been brought on by failure—either your own failures as a mother or your child's failures. Admitting your failure is the first step in facilitating hope and change. You might be tempted to think that confronting your sin and failure will produce more discouragement, but Scripture teaches that "he who conceals his sins does not prosper, but whoever confesses and renounces them finds mercy" (Prov. 28:13). It also says, "Blessed are those who mourn, for they will be comforted" (Matt. 5:4). God promises to console you when you are broken over your sin. You will actually be more confident and more capable of dealing with your child's failures if you take steps to humble yourself and deal with your own sin. As Jesus said, before you inspect the speck in your neighbor's eye, you must pay attention to the plank in your own eye (Matt. 7:3–5). Jesus knew it would be your tendency, as it is all people's, to minimize your own sin while focusing on your child's sin.

If you humble yourself and confess your sin to your child, you can fulfill your parental responsibilities with a clear conscience. Furthermore, a child's heart often is softened toward parental discipline when the child sees his parent's brokenness. But if you continue to rebuke or discipline your child when you have knowingly and willingly sinned against him without first seeking reconciliation, you are not in a position to discipline biblically and will most likely provoke him to anger.

Making a good confession takes thoughtful prayer and practice. If you are not in the habit of confessing your sins to your child, it might be difficult at first. Don't be dismayed; practice is a prerequisite for progress. And given your sin nature, there will be plenty of opportunities to practice! You might ask, "What is involved in making a good confession?" First, make a list of your sins and failures. Fully disclose to the Lord your transgressions: your sinful motives, attitudes, thoughts, actions, and words. Confession means that you agree with God and what he says in the Scriptures concerning your wrongdoing. This should encourage you; you are not telling God anything he does not already know! Then ask his forgiveness. "If we confess our sins, he is faithful and just and will forgive us our sins and purify us from all unrighteousness" (1 John 1:9). When God forgives, he chooses to remember your sins no more. The Bible tells us,

> For as high as the heavens are above the earth,
>   so great is his love for those who fear him;
> as far as the east is from the west,
>   so far has he removed our transgressions from us.
>   (Ps. 103:11–12)

The punishment for your sins has already been paid for by the Lord Jesus Christ; leave your guilt at the cross too. Remember, "there is now no condemnation for those who are in Christ Jesus" (Rom. 8:1).

Next, go to your child and thoroughly confess the sins you've committed against him without blame shifting or excuse making. It is possible that your child also may be guilty of sin and may even have provoked your sin. In time you will have to deal with your child's sin, but now is the time to take one hundred percent responsibility for your own sin! Tell your child that you are committing to a path of biblical change.[2] Tell him how you intend to change. If appropriate, ask your child to help you make these changes.[3] A true, heartfelt confession demands repentance. Repentance is turning away from, or "putting off," your sinful ways and turning toward, or "putting on," new righteous ways. God expects more than just lip service from your confession. He demands that you take your sin seriously and deal with it seriously. And he promises grace (supernatural help from heaven) for those who humble themselves and do so. If you don't begin making progress in correcting your habitual weakness, you will continue to be plagued with discouragement. You can tell yourself all day long that you have been forgiven, but if you know you will commit the same sin tomorrow, the guilt you feel will linger like a vulture hovering over a carcass. You will feel guilty today about what you know you will do wrong tomorrow. In other words, if you commit to biblical change but don't make a sincere effort to change, you will live under the burden of your own hypocrisy. Your children will also quickly learn to spot your hypocrisy. Whatever it takes, get help to change!

Finally, determine to make confessing sin and seeking forgiveness a regular practice in your parenting life. Confession and forgiveness should be the norm in every Christian home.

2. Along with the list you made enumerating your sins, it would be wise to consider carefully what ruling desires and idolatrous lusts are capturing your heart. Ask God to help you develop a comprehensive plan to mortify your fleshly desires and to put on righteous desires. Be prepared to share with your child at least some of the measures you plan to take. This will show your child that you are serious about your sin and give him hope that you are committed to change.

3. If your child is characterized by obedience and respect, then it is appropriate to ask him for help. Teach your child how to respectfully reprove you when you sin against him. Tell him how he can best help you to overcome sinful habits.

"Will you please forgive me?" and "I forgive you" should be words that easily roll off your lips because they express the true desire of your heart. If you find yourself choking on these words, finding it difficult to utter them without gagging, it might be a manifestation of a proud heart. Ask the Lord to give you a humble heart so that you might receive his grace. You can meditate on and pray James 4:6b–10.

> "God opposes the proud
>   but gives grace to the humble."
>
> Submit yourselves, then, to God. Resist the devil, and he will flee from you. Come near to God and he will come near to you. Wash your hands, you sinners, and purify your hearts, you double-minded. Grieve, mourn and wail. Change your laughter to mourning and your joy to gloom. Humble yourselves before the Lord, and he will lift you up.

At this point you might be thinking, "I have so many areas to deal with in my own life; how can I possibly begin to deal with my child's issues?" Good question. However, your imperfections don't disqualify you from parental service. Amazingly, God calls sinful mothers and fathers to bear and train the next generation of his church. This is God's normal means of passing the faith on from one generation to the next: big sinners helping little sinners see Jesus. After all, when God made his covenant with Abraham in Genesis 15 and 17, it was not due to Abraham's goodness but to God's grace. Just as God extended his covenant to Abraham's children, he extends it your children too. In 1 Corinthians 7:14 we are told that children of a believing parent are holy or set apart by the Lord. Good parenting is not based on your perfection, but on the goodness of God. Your child has the privilege of being raised in a home where Christ is exalted by precept and example. His grace is most vividly displayed in your weaknesses (2 Cor. 12:9).

As much as you may desire to parent perfectly, you obviously don't (and can't) parent out of perfection. You are not God. He alone is the perfect parent. But even though he *is* the perfect parent, his adopted children (you and me) struggle with sin and failure, too! It is God's desire to use ordinary, imperfect moms like you and me to accomplish the extraordinary purpose of building a legacy of faith for him. "But we have this treasure in jars of clay to show that this all-surpassing power is from God and not from us" (2 Cor. 4:7). Confess your sins and repent of them, but don't focus more on your failures than on the incredible, unmerited grace of God that both covers your sin and enables you to change (Rom. 5:20). The practice of holiness is a lifelong pursuit.

Whatever personal parenting failures are in your past, God intends for you to repent of your sin and then continue to faithfully teach and train your child in his ways. I marvel at my Redeemer when I consider how he alone can use my sin and its consequences for his glory, my good, and even the good of my children. Because of grace, your failures can actually prove to be more valuable than your victories. My dear sister, no amount of bad parenting is going to disqualify your child from heaven, and no amount of good parenting will gain it for him.

It is difficult to mesh the sovereignty of God—his absolute rule—with the responsibility of man. While God is pleased to use biblical parenting as a means to bring children to faith, his arm is not shortened by your unfaithfulness. He will accomplish all his purposes concerning your children. At the same time, you are responsible to the Lord and will be held accountable for your faithfulness in parenting according to the Scriptures. God calls you to be a faithful steward of your children, showing them Jesus every day and teaching them to observe all he has commanded (Deut. 6:4–9; Matt. 28:19–20). It is no use to dwell on your past mistakes or even your successes. God aims for you to press on.

If your own sin were all you had to deal with, it would be bad enough. But the problem gets even worse. Your sin is compounded by the sin of your darling children. (I mean "darling" in the most sincere way! No matter how sinful, they remain dear to us.) Your child is a sinner. Sin is bound in his heart. He came into this world a sinner, and he will remain a sinner until death. His sin should not surprise you—in fact, you should expect it! And until the Holy Spirit sets him free from the penalty and power of sin, he is a prisoner to it (Ps. 51:5; Prov. 22:15; Gal. 3:22). I remember calling a mentor of mine years ago to complain about my children's incessant sinning. My wiser friend reminded me, "Brenda, your children are sinners. Don't be surprised when they are rebellious and disobedient. Rather, be surprised when they are not!" That was quite a perspective shift for me.

Your child's propensity toward sin is not the only struggle you must encounter; there is often the frustration of his maturity level. It is important to have a firmly fixed and biblical perspective on your child's maturation. I have heard it said that our children are not just human beings, but "human becomings." The apostle Paul said, "When I was a child, I talked like a child, I thought like a child, I reasoned like a child. When I became a man, I put childish ways behind me" (1 Cor. 13:11). Children do not think or reason like adults. Even once they go through puberty and have the physical appearance of adults, they often lack maturity.

Wisdom dictates that you take into account and bear with your child's overall maturity, in the physical, emotional, social, and spiritual realms. Immaturity often appears as childishness. You might find the childishness of your children as maddening as their foolishness,[4] but you must not treat it

4. *Foolishness* is disobedience to God's Word.

like sin! I find this dynamic at work with my boys, who on any given day would give the WWF (World Wrestling Federation) something to talk about! The grabbing, squealing, pushing, pulling, and loud laughter can send my blood pressure skyward simply because it gets on my nerves! Of course, like any other childish behavior, it can become foolishness when one of them crosses the line from play to sinful anger. You cannot let your child's immaturity be an excuse for him to sin, and you must teach your child to put childish ways behind him as he matures. But you must also learn to be patient with your child's immaturities while he is growing up. One question I ask myself to help discern childishness from foolishness is, "Where is the sin?" If there is no sin on his part, I know it is probably a matter of childishness. If my child is not in sin, then I have to recognize that the sin is mine! I might be impatient or irritated because I am the sinner. This often means that I need to overlook the matter or bear with my child. If I can biblically identify his actions as sin, however, then I have to deal with it accordingly.

Unfortunately, you can't wait for your child to grow up in hopes that his foolishness will go away. In fact, the Bible warns that a child left to himself will become even more foolish (Prov. 29:15)! As your child matures, his sin may take on more subtle forms and he may become craftier in his sin. But make no mistake: left unhindered, his foolishness will accelerate. You must deal with your child's sin in the way the Scriptures prescribe. "A wise son brings joy to his father, but a foolish son grief to his mother" (Prov. 10:1). It is understandable that your child's sin will produce sadness, but you cannot allow this sadness to fill your heart and keep you from obedience to God. When you get right down to it, parenting is your response to God! How can you honor God and biblically deal with your child's repeated folly?

Steps toward Change

Step 1: You can pray for and with your child. Your best parenting efforts are futile apart from divine intervention. God alone can change a sinner's heart. Your child is in desperate need of an "inside job"—the transforming work of the Holy Spirit. Pray that your child comes to faith and repentance. Pray for God to place his seal, the Holy Spirit, upon your child. And once your child embraces Christ, never, ever quit praying! I have heard it said that prayer is like breathing—while inhaling and exhaling, let your prayers be unceasing (1 Thess. 5:17). Don't miss divine opportunities to pray *with* your child. This is profitable for two important reasons. First, it is a very practical way of modeling dependence on God. Your child will benefit greatly as he sees and hears you call on your heavenly Father with reverence and confidence. Second, just as Jesus taught his disciples to pray (Matt. 6:9–15), you should give your "disciple" a pattern for prayer as well. Left to himself, your child will probably pray in a self-centered and self-serving manner. Thus, you should model biblical prayers that exalt the greatness of God, communicate thankfulness to him, demonstrate how to seek his forgiveness, and show how and what to petition him for, especially regarding kingdom causes. As soon as your child is old enough to speak, have him mimic your prayers by repeating after you. Teach your child how to confess his sin before the Lord and ask for forgiveness. Teach him how to petition the Lord for saving and sustaining grace. Finally, listen to his prayers. As your child matures, his spoken prayers can become a window into his heart. Where does he struggle? What are the concerns of his heart? How does he view God? How he talks to God can help you discern his spiritual hunger and struggles.

Step 2: Commit to a path of biblical child training. Do you know the goals of Christian parenting? Are you prepared to use the Scriptures to teach, convict, correct, and train your child in

God's ways (2 Tim. 3:16–17)? It is not within the scope of this little booklet to teach on biblical parenting goals and methods; however, I must warn you to be wary of parenting materials that purport to be Christian but are merely smattered with Christian jargon. If your goals and methods are not in the Bible or cannot be deduced from the Bible, then they are not truly Christian. Any author or book that does not acknowledge and rely solely on the authority and sufficiency of the Scriptures cannot be trusted. As a Christian counselor, I encounter moms (even well-meaning Christian moms) who have been led astray by following the newest parenting fads. Our culture is drawn to the latest and greatest ideas, but as a Christian mother, you need only to commit yourself to following Christ and his Word. "This is what the LORD says: 'Stand at the crossroads and look; ask for the ancient paths, ask where the good way is, and walk in it, and you will find rest for your souls'" (Jer. 6:16). You should not expect God to bless ways that are contrary to his Word, regardless of what any "expert" says. "There is a way that seems right to a man, but in the end it leads to death" (Prov. 14:12). You can rejoice that God promises to give wisdom generously to all who ask without finding fault (James 1:5). No, you won't have the experience to know how to respond in every situation before it occurs. You will be caught off guard at times. You will make your share of unwise decisions. You will react sinfully on occasion. Oh, the graciousness of God to offer you wisdom time and time again, regardless of your mistakes! There is no need to flounder in your faults. If you acknowledge the Lord in all your parenting endeavors, he will make your paths straight.

Step 3: Be more concerned with your child's heart than with his behavior. Your child is not a robot who can be programmed to obey you automatically. Even if you could program his behavior, you would only be producing a Pharisee. Jesus said of the Pharisees, "You are like whitewashed tombs, which look beautiful on the outside but on the inside are full of dead men's bones and everything unclean. In the same way, on the outside you appear to people as righteous but on the inside you are full of hypocrisy and wickedness" (Matt. 23:27–28). The primary root of all your child's failures is his blackened heart. You may not like viewing your child this way, but unless you understand this to be the core problem, not only will you be continually frustrated by his failures, you will also lose focus on his greatest need—a new heart! Your job is not only to help your child see the error of his behavior but, more importantly, to help him examine his motives. "All a man's ways seem innocent to him, but motives are weighed by the LORD" (Prov. 16:2). Help your child to see the *why* behind his actions. Help him to understand the ruling desires of his heart (James 4:1–3).

Remember, your child is a little (or big) sinner who is in desperate need of the Savior. All of his failures are opportunities to point him to the cross. "Pointing" is not a passive proposition, but rather an active pursuit. Often, God's grace is magnified in the midst of your child's failures. Don't miss the occasion to share the good news of Jesus during these teachable moments. It is easy to lose sight of the unseen spiritual elements in the battle for your child's heart, but make no mistake—they are real (Eph. 6:12). Parenting is no peaceful pastime; it's warfare! How many battles have you experienced with your two-, ten-, or twenty-year-old?

Until the power of the gospel has changed your child's heart, leading him in righteousness will be especially difficult, "for what do righteousness and wickedness have in common? Or what fellowship can light have with darkness?" (2 Cor. 6:14). Paul's words in Romans more clearly explain the difficulty you may be facing.

> Those who live according to the sinful nature have their minds set on what that nature desires; but those who live in accordance with the Spirit have their minds set on what the Spirit desires.

The mind of sinful man is death, but the mind controlled by the Spirit is life and peace; the sinful mind is hostile to God. It does not submit to God's law, nor can it do so. (Rom. 8:5–7)

What does the man desire who is controlled by the sinful nature? To please self and to rule others. What does the man desire who is controlled by the Spirit? To please God and to serve others. If the sinful mind is hostile to God, it stands to reason that it will be hostile toward God's representative. You are Christ's ambassador, and you have the distinguished privilege of commending the King of Kings and his kingdom to your child every day (2 Cor. 5:20). Don't be dissuaded by your child's lack of interest or his hostility; keep pointing him to Jesus! Your direct influence is for only a season, so make the most of each moment.

Step 4: Even if your child has embraced Christ as his Lord and Savior, be patient with his progress. While you have been charged with watering, fertilizing, and pruning this tender sapling, God is the only one who can cause growth (1 Cor. 3:7). Consider your own spiritual growth—how long has it taken you to learn contentment, submission, self-control, and so on? And how much further do you have to go? Perhaps bishop J. C. Ryle said it best: "We must not expect too much from our hearts in this life. Sinners we were when we began this road, sinners we shall find we continue: renewed, pardoned, justified certainly—yet sinners to the very last."[5] If your child is truly born again, you can take great comfort in knowing that God will be faithful to complete the good work he has begun in your child's heart[6] (Rom. 8:30; Phil. 1:6)!

5. J. C. Ryle, *Aspects of Holiness* (London: Grace Publications Trust, 1999), 29.
6. When your child becomes regenerate is not always easy to determine. But any true conversion, regardless of the age of the person, is accompanied by a sensitivity to sin and a desire for the things of God. Don't rush your child into saying the "sinner's prayer" and then assume that this makes him saved. Your child's prayer does not save him; God does. Look for the work of the Spirit in the life of your child. Continue to evangelize your child until you are confident that he is demonstrating the fruit of the Spirit in increasing measure.

Maximizing Your Mothering Struggles:
A Right View of Trials

Since struggle is inevitable, make the most of it! God uses external pressures to reveal internal priorities. Parental exasperation can be a catalyst for profitable introspection.[7] Introspection is the inspection of what's going on inside your heart. It's an examination or checkup of sorts. Your difficulty is an occasion to take a personal spiritual inventory. The Puritan Thomas Watson wrote, "Affliction teaches us to know ourselves. In prosperity we are for the most part strangers to ourselves. God makes us know affliction, that we may better know ourselves. We see that corruption in our hearts in the time of affliction, which we would not believe was there."[8] In times of ease you might be tempted to think that your faith is mature, but it is in times of trouble that the measure of your faith is proven. The Scripture says, "Do not think of yourself more highly than you ought, but rather think of yourself with sober judgment, in accordance with the measure of faith God has given you" (Rom. 12:3). When trouble comes, it puts the squeeze on your heart, and whatever is in your heart will be revealed in your words, your actions, and your attitudes. Even your motives will become more apparent.

James says that all our trials are designed to bring about spiritual maturity. In other words, don't waste your trials. Your mothering mayhem is a means to further your sanctification. "Consider it pure joy, my brothers, whenever you face trials of many kinds, because you know that the testing of your faith develops perseverance. Perseverance must finish its work so that you may be mature and complete, not lacking anything" (James 1:2–4). This way of thinking challenges your natural

7. In contrast, morbid introspection is a preoccupation with your shortcomings and is not profitable. All self-examination should lead you to a greater view of God's grace and mercy and thus inspire gratitude and greater service to the Lord.

8. Thomas Watson, *All Things for Good* (1663; repr., Edinburgh: Banner of Truth Trust, 1991), 28–29.

assumption that where there are trials, there is misery. Because you are a Christian mother, God wants you to think differently about your trials. Romans 8:28 says, "And we know that in all things God works for the good of those who love him, who have been called according to his purpose." This is not a cliché; it is a promise! God is up to something really good in the midst of your trouble—he is conforming you more and more into the image of Christ! In the end, that will be worth every conceivable trial you could ever face.

You might be thinking, "How do I go from thinking about my trial as misery to thinking about it as joy?" Great question! It begins in your redeemed mind. James exhorts, "Consider it pure joy." This is an imperative, not merely a suggestion. He boldly states it as a command, and as such, you can obey it! You can choose to think about your trials from God's point of view, or you can simmer in your own self-defeating thoughts and set a course that not only promises negative consequences, but also does not please the Lord. "Considering" is not a passive response to your current struggle, but a purposeful thought process whereby you instruct your heart. Another Bible translation says, "Count it all joy" (ESV). This is a deliberate act to recall and enumerate God's good purposes and promises in the midst of any given trial. The battle begins in your mind. How will you think about your difficulty? How will you counsel yourself? God wants you to bring your thoughts captive to the obedience of Christ (2 Cor. 10:5). You can learn to have the mind of Christ (1 Cor. 2:6–16)! Ask God to help you.

Your prayer may sound something like this: "Dear Lord, you tell me that I can *choose* to be joyful even though I am feeling overwhelmed, spent, and discouraged. While I confess that I would prefer ease to adversity, I thank you for giving me exactly what I need in order to become more like Jesus. I can be joyful when I focus on all the ways you are using my present trial to mature my faith, and I can rejoice when I remember that every promise in the Scripture is as good as done! Please give me wisdom to know how to persevere and mature in this trial." It can be very beneficial to make a list of all the ways you see God working in your life, your husband's life, your marriage, your child's life, and even the lives of others as a result of your current difficulty. Also, keep a list of God's promises that pertain to you and your problems so you can meditate on them day and night. Keep these lists handy to pray over and think about when you're tempted to give in to "stinkin' thinkin'." Choose to be continually transformed by the renewing of your mind (Rom. 12:2).

Another way to maximize the benefits of your trials is to recognize the opportunity to grow in wisdom. "If any of you lacks wisdom, he should ask God, who gives generously to all without finding fault" (James 1:5). Wisdom is the skill of living in a fallen world to the glory of Christ. How do you attain wisdom? Through a greater knowledge of God. "His divine power has given us everything we need for life and godliness through our knowledge of him" (2 Peter 1:3). I can't even begin to say how many truths have been written on my heart as a result of a direct and desperate plea to God regarding some issue with my children. I have been highly motivated to dig deep into God's Word when I am wrestling to lead my children to greater knowledge of God and his ways. God bids you to ask for wisdom when you encounter various kinds of trials; this certainly includes parenting concerns. Then he demonstrates his lavish love and great patience by offering wisdom despite your past failings.

Spiritual maturity is produced when you ask God for wisdom, trust him at his word, and obey him. Unfortunately, we often doubt God's word and put more credence in our own feelings and experiences. James warns against such tendencies: "But when he asks [for wisdom], he must believe and not doubt, because he who doubts is like a wave of the sea, blown and tossed by the wind. That man should not think he will receive anything from the Lord; he is a double-minded man, unstable in all he does" (James 1:6–8). The sin of unbelief is a serious matter.

Anything short of taking God at his word is unbelief. God does not bless unbelief! When you allow your feelings or experiences, rather than the objective word of God, to dictate your parenting practices, you are building toward a tsunami. The winds of your present emotions and past experiences will blow like a mighty storm seeking to steer you off course—or, worse yet, to leave you capsized. Only the authoritative and inerrant Word of God can keep you steady through life's storms. This is not to say that your feelings and experiences don't matter, but they must not take precedence over God's Word.

How do you choke out the seeds of doubt that are sure to sprout in your heart? How do you fully place your trust in God's Word and his ways? You do it by making one right decision at a time. "He who trusts in himself is a fool, but he who walks in wisdom is kept safe" (Prov. 28:26). In order to walk, you must take one step at a time. This is also true in the spiritual realm. Ask yourself, "What is the *next* step that God wants me to take?" and do it! As the beautiful old hymn says, "Trust and obey, for there's no other way to be happy in Jesus, but to trust and obey."[9]

Perhaps you are thinking, "I know God's Word is supposed to be the absolute rule for my life, but in the heat of the battle I often lose faith. I just can't seem to be obedient." If you are a Christian, yes you can—and you must! You are without excuse. You have far more reason to believe than generations before you. "Now faith is being sure of what we hope for and certain of what we do not see. This is what the ancients were commended for" (Heb. 11:1–2). The Old Testament saints took God at his word with no Savior and no New Testament; no wonder they were commended! You must have a high view of God's Word if you are going to trust not only your own life to it, but your child's life as well. My dear friend, please don't miss this: God's Word is fully trustworthy because it contains the very words of God (2 Peter 1:20–21).

9. John H. Sammis, "Trust and Obey" (1887), in *Trinity Hymnal*, rev. ed. (Suwanee, GA: Great Commission Publications, 1990), no. 672.

One of my favorite stories in the gospels is the cry of a distressed parent who struggled with fully trusting Christ.

> A man in the crowd answered, "Teacher, I brought you my son, who is possessed by a spirit that has robbed him of speech. Whenever it seizes him, it throws him to the ground. He foams at the mouth, gnashes his teeth and becomes rigid. I asked your disciples to drive out the spirit, but they could not."
>
> "O unbelieving generation," Jesus replied, "how long shall I stay with you? How long shall I put up with you? Bring the boy to me."
>
> So they brought him. When the spirit saw Jesus, it immediately threw the boy into a convulsion. He fell to the ground and rolled around, foaming at the mouth.
>
> Jesus asked the boy's father, "How long has he been like this?"
>
> "From childhood," he answered. "It has often thrown him into fire or water to kill him. But if you can do anything, take pity on us and help us."
>
> "'If you can'?" said Jesus. "Everything is possible for him who believes."
>
> Immediately the boy's father exclaimed, "I do believe; help me overcome my unbelief!" (Mark 9:17–24)

I've never had to deal with a demon-possessed child (although some have certainly seemed like it to me), but I have read God's Word and struggled to believe it. I have echoed this father's cry on countless occasions: "Father, I believe; help me overcome my unbelief!" If your faith is weak, cry out to the Father. He will be pleased to make you an overcomer. In fact, that's the bonus of your trials. God is committed to placing tailor-made trials in your life so that you may overcome your flesh, the world, and Satan and become mature and complete, not lacking anything. When you are mature in Christ, you can best glorify the Father with your life. "These [trials] have come so that your faith—of greater worth than gold, which perishes even though refined by fire—may be proved genuine and may result in praise, glory and honor when Jesus Christ is revealed" (1 Peter 1:7).

Wrapping It Up

Maturity is promised to those who persevere (James 1:4). Perseverance is the ability to stay the course no matter what the obstacles. You must have a holy resolve to do all God asks of you, for as long as he asks, and trust him with the results. This steadfastness is not something you muster up within yourself, but rather it is the result of the resurrection power of Christ living in you through the Holy Spirit. You need perseverance to faithfully endure trials, and trials endured faithfully produce even greater perseverance. Galatians 6:9 is a hallmark verse for moms: "Let us not become weary in doing good, for at the proper time we will reap a harvest if we do not give up."

Fix firmly in your mind the fact that parenting is the ministry of repetition. It necessitates saying and doing the same things over and over again until your child gets it or until God releases you from the job! Paul wrote to the Philippians, "It is no trouble for me to write the same things to you again, and it is a safeguard for you" (Phil. 3:1). You don't know which time the light may go on in your child's heart or head, so don't give up. In fact, you don't have the option of quitting. Christian mothering is not for quitters!

Thankfully, the Lord has not left you without resources to help you persevere. If you are married, your husband can be a major motivator to help you fight your daily battles. Regularly communicate with him regarding the struggles you frequently deal with. (Don't forget to share the encouragements too!) Ask for his input in resolving mothering issues. Often, he will see the situation from a different perspective that will allow him to shed light on an otherwise dim matter. Mine your husband's wisdom on how to best handle the discipline of your child. This can be really helpful when you lack confidence in your mothering abilities. I can remember a particularly difficult situation with my daughter. I was fearful about following through with the discipline we had established for her. Yet I was able to push past my fears by focusing on my responsibility before God to submit to my husband. There is confidence in submission! Enlist your husband to be active in instruction and discipline when he is home. Mothers often become the "parenting experts" because of their close relationship with their children. Help your husband to become a great father by modeling biblical parenting for him if necessary, and by lovingly drawing him into the parenting process.

Some of you are thinking, "My husband is one of the reasons I'm so discouraged! He doesn't help me with the children at all. What am I to do?" First of all, you need to determine if this is an indication of his lack of parental interest or if there is a bigger marital issue. How is your relationship with your husband? Would your husband say that you identify yourself more fully as a wife or as a mother? Despite all the pulls of motherhood, your husband should be your first human priority. Furthermore, don't make assumptions about your husband (don't, for example, sinfully judge him and his motives); rather, respectfully discuss your concerns with him and appeal to him for help. If your husband is unwilling to make progress in your marriage or accept his responsibility in the parenting process, perhaps you can persuade him to meet with you and your pastor or another more mature Christian couple.[10] If you cannot convince him to go with you for help, seek out your pastor, an elder, or an older godly woman to counsel you and help you stick with it.

That brings us to another means to help you persevere: the local church. The local church provides several key components

---

10. A biblical counselor could be of great value in this situation. But you need to make sure that the counsel will be from the Bible. You can go to www.nanc.org to find a biblical counselor in your area.

to strengthen you along life's journey. When you became a Christian, you were adopted into a new family—God's family (Eph. 1:5; 2:19). Your adoption affords you privileges and responsibilities in the family of God. God never intended for you to fly solo as a Christian or a mother. A healthy church will provide sound biblical teaching, accountability, fellowship with other like-minded moms, a venue to use your spiritual gifts, and protection. It can also be a place to find a mentor to help you work through your mothering madness. Look for a godly woman whose children are a little bit ahead of your own, and ask her for guidance. I am indebted to several older, godly women who have heard my cries of distress and returned those cries with solid biblical hope and instruction.

Final Words of Encouragement

It is easy to see the goodness of God when your child is a joy to you. But remember that in times of trouble your child is no less a gift from God. "Sons are a heritage from the LORD, children a reward from him" (Ps. 127:3). Not every woman is given the gift of a child; pray that you will not take the opportunity for granted. Paul called the Galatians "my dear children, for whom I am again in the pains of childbirth until Christ is formed in you" (Gal. 4:19). Do you remember your labor pains? Excruciating at times! But these pains were necessary to bring forth one of your most prized possessions: your child. Your biological pains are gone, but your spiritual pains will continue. You are now laboring to see your child born again in Christ. Labor is typically intensely difficult and painful work. Your ability to remain hopeful in your bleakest moments depends on how well you cultivate your walk with Christ.

The prerequisite to Christian parenting is a personal relationship with Jesus Christ through faith in his substitutionary death on the cross. You cannot pass on to your children what you do not possess yourself. Furthermore, as harsh as it may sound, a mother who has not trusted in Christ is doomed to discouragement. Apart from God, life does not, cannot, and will not have meaning. What is mothering apart from a divine duty? It is little more than a biological function and perhaps an attempt to raise a moral child who will ultimately be lost for eternity. If you are discouraged and don't know where to turn, turn to Jesus. He bids you to come and trust him alone for salvation, and he alone promises to give meaning to your life and motherhood. Your best mothering efforts will flow from your personal relationship with Jesus Christ. May the Lord grant you the enabling grace you need as Christ is formed in you through your mothering!

If you are like me, motherhood has cost you a few brain cells, and you may need a cheat sheet to remember the contents of this booklet. We've covered a lot of ground, so let's recap:

- Trials are to be expected in this sinful, fallen world. Trials can produce temptations to sin.
- No temptation is new. Your fight with discouragement is common to mothers throughout the ages.
- God is faithful to deliver you from your trial or to provide all you need to face the trial without sinning.
- Discouragement can result from your own failures. God will provide forgiveness for these failures, upon confession and repentance, and the wisdom and power to correct future failures.
- Discouragement can also come from your child's shortcomings. God expects you to treat your children with understanding, using biblical goals and methods. You are to be faithful in your stewardship regardless of the fruitfulness of your efforts. In other words, keep the faith!
- God's purpose in every trial is to mature your faith so that you may give him glory by looking more like Jesus

every day. Whatever promotes God's glory is for your ultimate good!

- You are to persevere and stay the course of Scripture in all your mothering issues by using God's Word as your guide and not trusting in your own feelings or experiences.
- All children are a gift from God, not just the easy or good ones!
- A vibrant personal relationship with Jesus Christ is the single most important factor in your mothering.

Allow me to leave you with one final thought to fix firmly in your mind: "Know therefore that the LORD your God is God; he is the faithful God, keeping his covenant of love to a thousand generations of those who love him and keep his commands" (Deut. 7:9). It is vital that you view your mothering under the umbrella of God's covenant promises. It is God's faithfulness that you must look to every day. He is the faithful God. Did you catch that? *Faithful* is more than what he does; it is who he is. In his book *Far as the Curse Is Found*, Michael Williams beautifully portrays God's heart for his people: "Yahweh is thus the covenant name for God: I am the one who keeps promise. I am the one who is always faithful. I am the one who is here for you. I am the one who acts in your behalf. In giving his name, God promises his covenant presence to his people. He might be saying, 'Call me Dad. I'm the one you can count on.' "[11] It is God's covenant promises that should motivate you to pray and work daily for your child's eternal security. A pastor friend of mine once said, "We don't presume upon the promise of God; rather, we work to teach, convict, correct, and train our children in the Scriptures precisely because of the promises of God!" Pray fervently, realizing that salvation is a gift from the Lord, but work diligently as if it all depended on you.

11. Michael D. Williams, *Far as the Curse Is Found* (Phillipsburg, NJ: P&R Publishing, 2005), 30.

Although there are biblical examples of covenant children who rejected the faith, God gives you many promises throughout his Word to encourage a hopeful optimism. One of my favorite passages is Malachi 2:15: "Has not the LORD made them one? In flesh and spirit they are his. And why one? Because he was seeking godly offspring. So guard yourself in your spirit, and do not break faith with the wife of your youth." Marriage is designed, in part, to produce worshipers of the living God. While many churches emphasize evangelizing those outside the covenant,[12] you will do well to remember that God's normal means for building his church is for one generation to pass the faith down to the next! As love for Christ and his kingdom is exalted in your home, you will become a spiritual magnet for your children and your children's children. The world will take notice of the beautiful lives produced by faith in Christ, and outsiders will undoubtedly be drawn to the gospel too. This is the privilege of a mother's calling: building the kingdom of God from the inside out!

12. I am not minimizing the efforts of churches to reach the lost, but only hope to emphasize that this should not be done to the neglect of our covenantal responsibilities. When we lovingly fulfill our duties within the covenant community, we become spiritual magnets for a lost and dying world.